American Indians of the West
Battling the Elements

Katelyn Rice

Consultants

Katie Blomquist, M.Ed.
Fairfax County Public Schools

Nicholas Baker, Ed. D.
Supervisor of Curriculum and Instruction
Colonial School District, DE

Vanessa Ann Gunther, Ph. D.
Department of History
Chapman University

Publishing Credits

Rachelle Cracchiolo, M.S.Ed., *Publisher*
Conni Medina, M.A.Ed., *Managing Editor*
Emily R. Smith, M.A.Ed., *Series Developer*
Diana Kenney, M.A.Ed., NBCT, *Content Director*
Johnson Nguyen, *Multimedia Designer*
Lynette Ordoñez, *Editor*

Image Credits: pp. 2–3, 10, 20, 22–23, 25, 32 North Wind Picture
Archives; p. 7 (top) Stocktrek Images, Inc./Alamy, (bottom) Nancy
Carter/North Wind Picture Archives; pp. 8–9 National Geographic
Image Collection/Alamy; p. 9 Richard Hook/Getty Images; p.13
(bottom) NativeStock/North Wind Picture Archives, (top) Nancy
Carter/North Wind; p.14 LOC [LC-USZ62-99798]; p. 17 Simon Speed/
Wikimedia Commons; p. 19 NativeStock/North Wind Picture Archives;
p. 21 Wikimedia Commons/Public Domain; pp. 16, back cover Walter
Siegmund/Wikimedia Commons; all other images from iStock
and/or Shutterstock.

Library of Congress Cataloging-in-Publication Data

Names: Rice, Katelyn, author.
Title: American Indians of the West: battling the elements / Katelyn
Rice.
Description: Huntington Beach, CA : Teacher Created Materials, 2016. |
  Includes index.
Identifiers: LCCN 2015051137 (print) | LCCN 2016000149 (ebook) | ISBN
  9781493830695 (pbk.) | ISBN 9781480756717 (eBook)
Subjects: LCSH: Indians of North America--West (U.S.)--History--
Juvenile
  literature.
Classification: LCC E78.W5 R525 2016 (print) | LCC E78.W5 (ebook) | DDC
  978.004/97--dc23
LC record available at http://lccn.loc.gov/2015051137

Teacher Created Materials
5301 Oceanus Drive
Huntington Beach, CA 92649-1030
http://www.tcmpub.com
ISBN 978-1-4938-3069-5

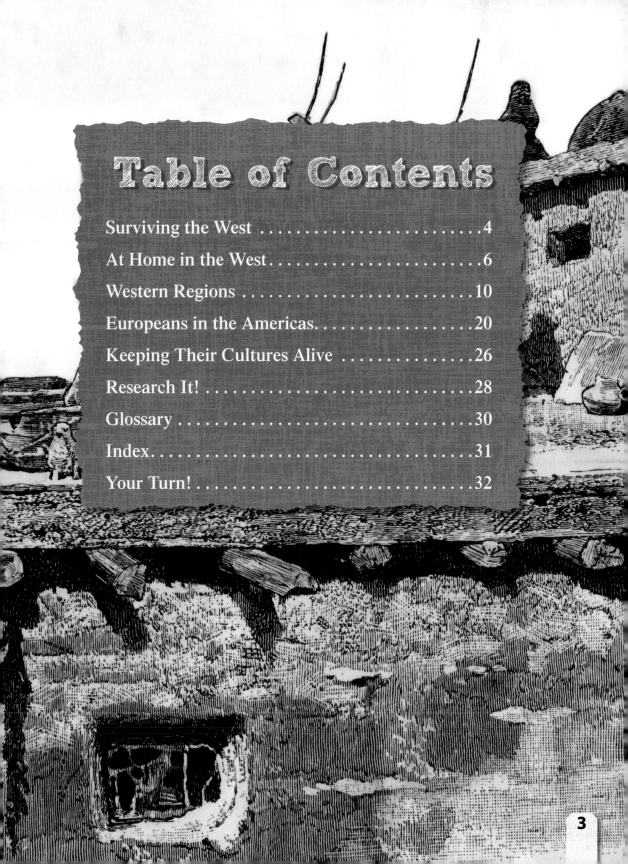

Table of Contents

Surviving the West

Wheeler Peak, Nevada

Long before Europeans found North and South America, millions of people already lived there. These people were American Indians. Their **ancestors** came to the area thousands of years ago. They lived in many different **tribes.** A tribe is a group of people who share a **culture**. Each tribe had its own traditions, beliefs, and ways of life.

American Indians lived in almost every part of North America. All western tribes had very different ways of life. This is because the West is a **diverse** region. There are towering mountains, dry deserts, fertile valleys, and miles of jagged coastline. It may seem difficult to live in some of these places. But, Western tribes found ways to thrive in all these environments.

Reynolds Mountain, Montana

North Cascades, Washington

Mojave Desert, California

At Home in the West

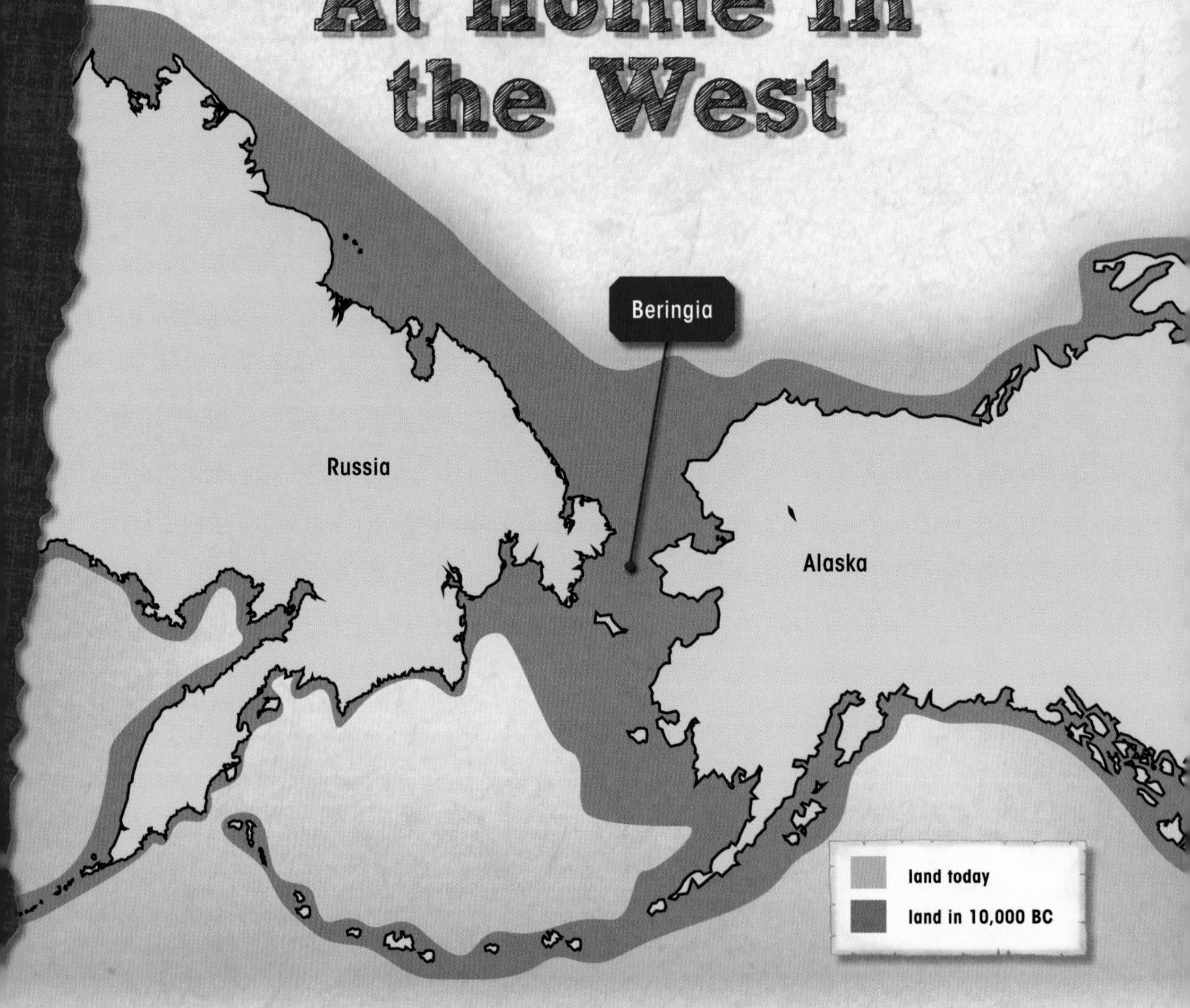

Beringia

Russia

Alaska

	land today
	land in 10,000 BC

During the last Ice Age, people began settling in North America. These people are called Paleo-Indians. They likely crossed a land bridge from Asia to North America. The bridge is called Beringia (buh-RIN-jee-uh). It is now covered by a body of water called the Bering Strait. By 10,000 BC, Paleo-Indians had spread throughout North and South America.

Paleo-Indians were **nomadic**. They did not stay in one place. They moved each season to follow herds of animals that they hunted. This ensured access to food.

woolly mammoths

saber-tooth cat

Paleo-Indians learned to use what was around them. They hunted animals that are now extinct, such as woolly mammoths and saber-tooth cats. They made tools out of wood, stone, and animal bones. They sharpened stones into points and put them on wooden spears. Later, they learned to make tools out of copper. They used furs and hides, or skins, to make clothing and to cover their homes. Paleo-Indians passed these skills on to their **descendants**—American Indians.

Paleo-Indians prepare a caribou to be eaten.

Early American Indians may or may not have named their tribes. But later, the tribes were given practical names. They were named after what they hunted, ate, or were known for making. One of these tribes from present-day Nevada is known as the Koop Ticutta. This name means "ground-squirrel eaters." They hunted squirrels by pouring water into a squirrel's burrow. When it fled its flooded home, they caught it. They also ate rabbits, fish, roots, and grasses.

ground squirrel in present-day Nevada

family inside a pit house

The Anasazi were the ancestors of the American Indians of the Southwest. They are from what is now Utah, Arizona, and New Mexico. They lived in that region from AD 100 to about AD 1600. The Anasazi lived in cliff dwellings. These dwellings are stacked homes built into the side of a cliff. The Anasazi also lived in caves and pit houses. Pit houses are round or square houses that are halfway underground. Their pit houses were made of grass, sticks, and dirt. Each house had a hole in the roof that allowed people to enter and exit. The hole also let out smoke when the people cooked inside. This living structure kept them safe from the harsh environment outside. The Anasazi skills and ideas were passed down through the years. Western tribes had learned to survive.

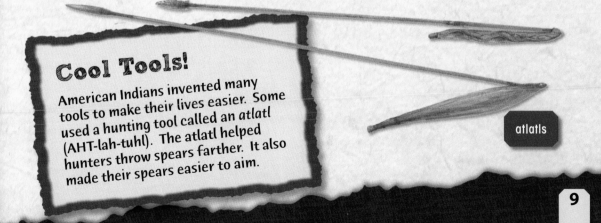

Cool Tools!

American Indians invented many tools to make their lives easier. Some used a hunting tool called an *atlatl* (AHT-lah-tuhl). The atlatl helped hunters throw spears farther. It also made their spears easier to aim.

atlatls

Western Regions

American Indians of the West lived in various regions. Those regions are the Southwest, the Great Basin, the Plateau (plah-TOH), the Pacific Northwest, and California. Each region has a **unique** climate. Tribes adapted their lifestyles to the regions in which they lived.

Pacific Northwest

Plateau

Great Basin

California

Southwest

Southwest

The Southwest is hot and dry for much of the year. It is mostly desert. Staying cool and conserving water is important when living in such a harsh climate. Among others, tribes in this region include the Hopi, Zuni, Taos, and Acoma.

Southwestern tribes built **pueblos**. The word *pueblo* means "village" in Spanish. Some pueblos were built above ground. Others were cliff dwellings. Both types of homes were made of stone and adobe (uh-DOH-bee). This kept the houses cool during scorching summer days. Many pueblo groups were linked through a series of roads. The roads made trading easier between groups.

Southwestern tribes grew crops, such as squash and corn. They also grew cotton to make into clothing. They developed a type of farming called *terrace farming*. Farms were built like a set of stairs. When it rained, water trickled from the top step all the way to the bottom. This design allowed people to water all of the plants on a farm with very little water.

Adobe

Adobe is a strong building material. To make it, Pueblo Indians mixed clay, sand, grass, and water. Then, they baked it in the sun for hours to make it hard like a brick. They stacked adobe bricks on top of one another to build walls. Wet adobe was placed between bricks and on the faces of the walls.

Great Basin

The Great Basin extends from Nevada and Utah into parts of Colorado, Oregon, Idaho, Wyoming, and even into parts of Arizona, California, and Montana. The Great Basin is a large desert. It seldom rains, and there are few areas with abundant plant and animal life. During the summers, there is blistering heat. But the winters can be bitterly cold. Tribes that lived in this region, such as the Paiute (PI-yoot), Shoshone (shuh-SHO-nee), Ute (YOOT), and Bannock, had to cope with this harsh environment.

Great Basin during winter

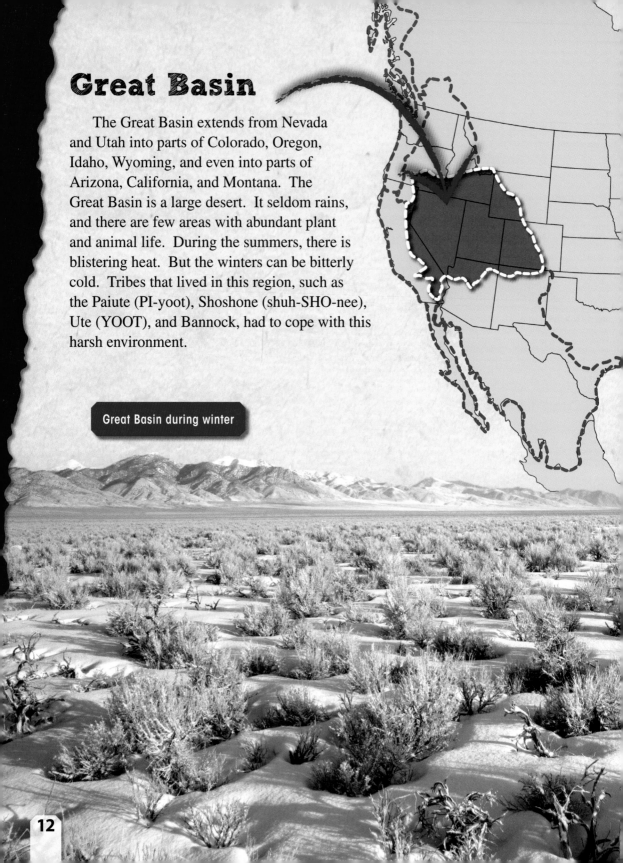

American Indians in the Great Basin were nomadic hunters and gatherers. They moved often to hunt animals. They used simple tools, such as bows and arrows, to catch animals such as antelope and jackrabbits. But these tribes mostly ate plants. Because farming is difficult in this region, tribes gathered berries, fruits, seeds, roots, and nuts to eat. These could be easily dried and stored for the winter months.

Homes in the Great Basin were usually **temporary**. Tribes built new homes after they moved. One type of shelter was a brush home. Brush homes were made from the branches of trees. More materials, such as bark or dirt, were added to shelters during the colder winter months.

Paiute brush home

Great Basin Basketry

Women made baskets to use when gathering food. The baskets were tightly woven with branches and bark from nearby trees. This ensured seeds could not fall through the cracks. Some baskets were woven so tightly that they could hold water!

Plateau

Nestled between the Great Plains, the Great Basin, and the Pacific Northwest is the Plateau region. It covers parts of Oregon, Washington, Idaho, Montana, and Canada. Tribes that lived there included the Nez Percé (PUHRS), Kutenai (KOO-tuh-nay), Flathead, and Modoc.

This region has warm summers and snowy winters. During the winter, Plateau tribes lived in villages. There, families made pit houses or mat-covered homes. Pit houses were made of wooden posts that were tied at the top with strips of bark. A fire was lit in the center for warmth. The smoke escaped through a hole at the top. Mat-covered houses were cone-shaped. They were wrapped with a reed called *tule* (TOO-lee). Tribes also had smaller camps set up around the area to live in during the other seasons. This was more convenient for hunting and gathering.

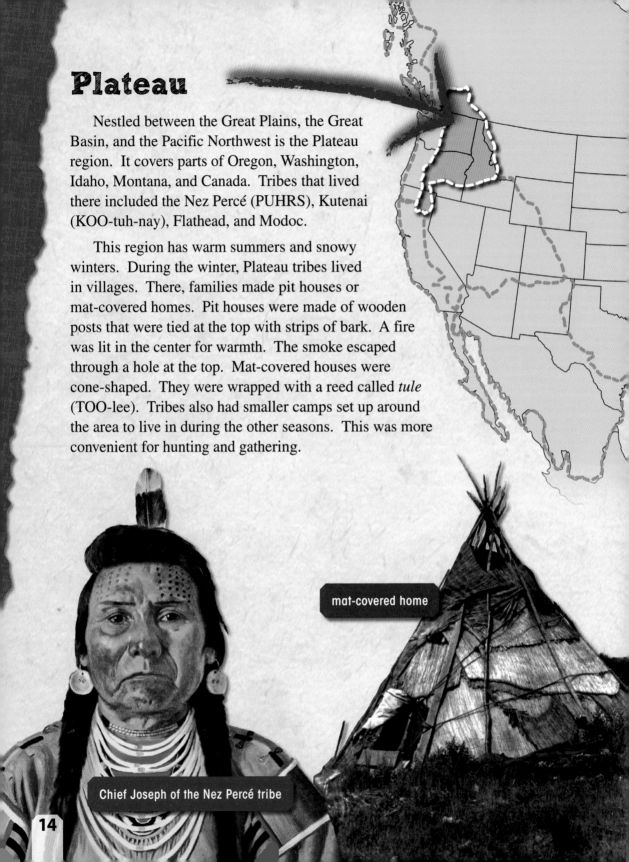

mat-covered home

Chief Joseph of the Nez Percé tribe

14

Hunting and gathering was a way of life for the Plateau Indians. During spring, roots were gathered. In the fall, women and children gathered berries. Tribes also tracked animals, such as deer and elk. Since Plateau tribes settled near water, they also fished. They used spears, traps, and nets to catch salmon, trout, and other fish in local rivers.

Nez Percé woman and her son

Trade Routes

The region's rivers and central location helped tribes trade with one another. The people used canoes to travel short distances and carry goods.

Pacific Northwest

Pacific Northwest tribes lived in northern California, Oregon, Washington, Canada, and southeastern Alaska. Many tribes called this region home, including the Makah, Umpqua (UHMP-kwah), Nootka, Chinook (shuh-NUHK), and Cowlitz. Tribes in this cold and rainy region stayed close to the ocean, which provided most of their food.

People ate seafood, such as salmon, whale, and sea otter. They also hunted deer and moose. To hunt, they sharpened rocks into arrowheads. They fastened the arrowheads to branches to make spears. Sometimes, they caught fish using handmade nets.

With ample food, people in this region lived in permanent homes called *longhouses*. Some were 200 feet long and could house as many as 60 people! Longhouses were often two stories tall. The second story was used as a sleeping area. Trees are abundant in this region. So longhouses were made of wooden planks.

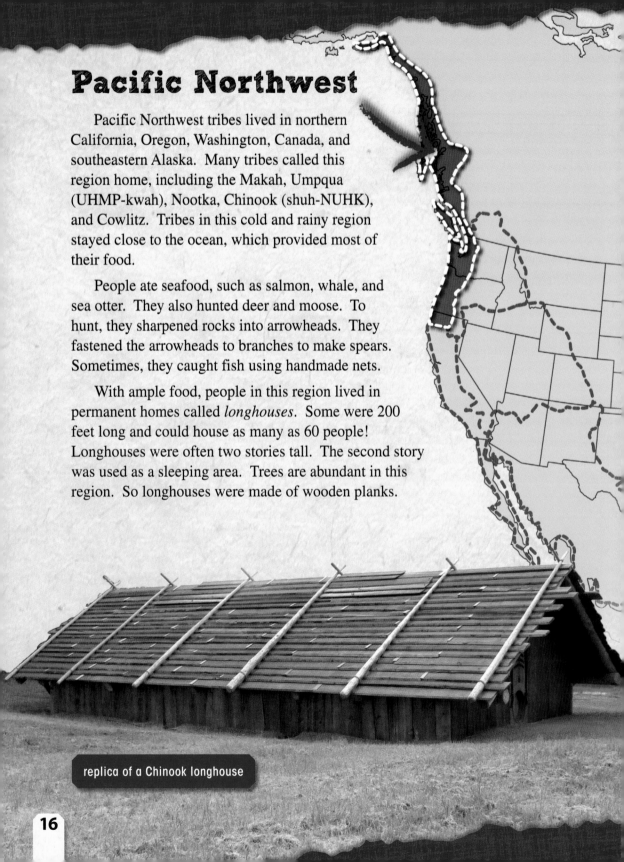

replica of a Chinook longhouse

Pacific Northwestern tribes carved many things out of wood, too. They made instruments, such as drums, flutes, and rattles. They made masks for religious ceremonies. But they are best known for their wooden totem poles. These are logs with animals and faces carved into them. Totem poles were used to mark important events and tell family histories. They were also used for religious purposes.

totem pole

string made from whale sinew

Nothing Wasted

Whales were an important source of food. But tribes also used whale sinew as thread. Sinew is a strong tissue that connects muscle to bone. They used whale oil to flavor food and to keep fires going in the rain.

California

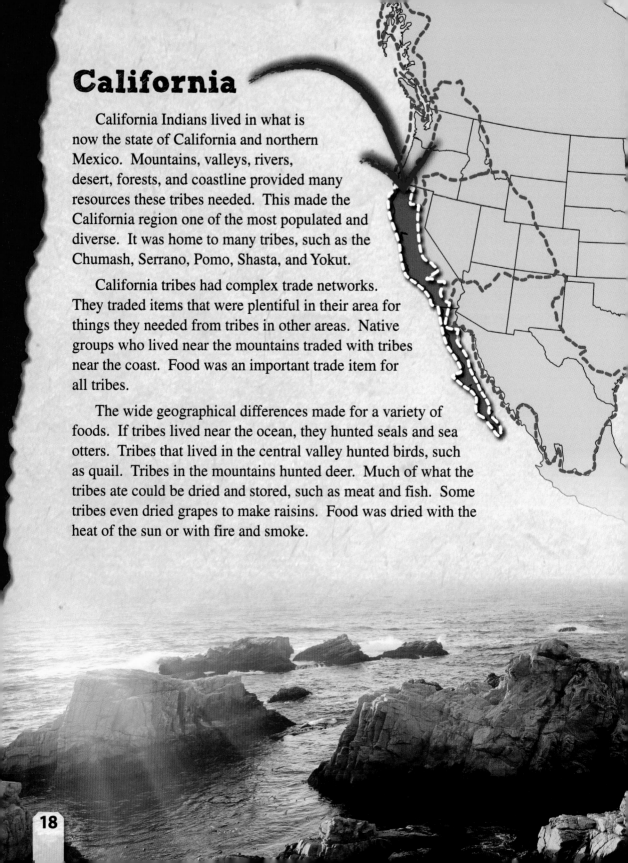

California Indians lived in what is now the state of California and northern Mexico. Mountains, valleys, rivers, desert, forests, and coastline provided many resources these tribes needed. This made the California region one of the most populated and diverse. It was home to many tribes, such as the Chumash, Serrano, Pomo, Shasta, and Yokut.

California tribes had complex trade networks. They traded items that were plentiful in their area for things they needed from tribes in other areas. Native groups who lived near the mountains traded with tribes near the coast. Food was an important trade item for all tribes.

The wide geographical differences made for a variety of foods. If tribes lived near the ocean, they hunted seals and sea otters. Tribes that lived in the central valley hunted birds, such as quail. Tribes in the mountains hunted deer. Much of what the tribes ate could be dried and stored, such as meat and fish. Some tribes even dried grapes to make raisins. Food was dried with the heat of the sun or with fire and smoke.

Durable Homes

The materials California Indians used to build their houses varied, depending on their location. Tribes near the coast built grass mat houses. Tribes in forested areas built cedar bark lodges.

cedar bark lodge

Appetizing Acorns

Acorns were very important to California tribes. Acorns were dried for one year. Then, they were ground into meal, which is similar to flour. From this, acorn "chips" were made or the flour was boiled and eaten. The mush that resulted had the consistency of pudding.

Europeans in the Americas

In the late 1400s, the Age of Discovery began. Europeans wanted to find faster trade routes to Asia. Traders traveled mainly on land. It took months for them to travel the long roads. And it was dangerous, too. Thieves often attacked traders along the way. All of this made goods from Asia very expensive. Explorers set out to find new routes to Asia by sea.

Traders travel between Europe and Asia along the Silk Road.

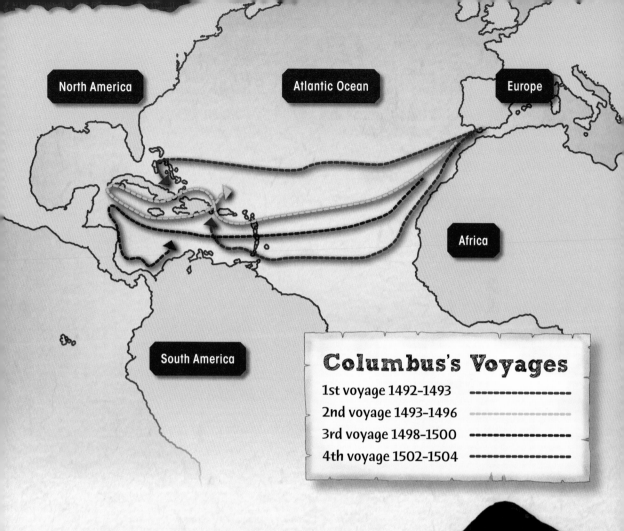

North America

Atlantic Ocean

Europe

Africa

South America

Columbus's Voyages

1st voyage 1492–1493	-------------------
2nd voyage 1493–1496	-------------------
3rd voyage 1498–1500	-------------------
4th voyage 1502–1504	-------------------

In 1492, Christopher Columbus sailed west from Spain. He and his crew landed in the Caribbean. But he thought that he had landed near India. Even though he landed in the Caribbean, he called the people he met there Indians. And the name stuck.

Soon, Europeans came to understand that there were two continents between the Atlantic and Pacific Oceans. It was not long before they saw financial **opportunity** in these new continents. Many countries began claiming land in the Americas. Since this land was new to Europeans, they called it the New World.

Christopher Columbus

Europeans and American Indians began trading for many different goods. Europeans traded coffee, wheat, rice, bananas, pigs, cattle, and more. In return, tribes traded things, such as furs, corn, tomatoes, pumpkins, potatoes, and tobacco. This exchange of goods became known as the **Columbian Exchange**.

American Indians trade with Europeans.

Through this exchange, many tribes received horses. Tribes had not seen horses until the Europeans brought horses to the New World. Horses changed the American Indians' way of life. Horses helped tribes plow their fields. They let tribes travel farther and faster. Horses helped them hunt large animals. Horses became important to many tribes.

But as Europeans traded with the tribes, they also shared something else—diseases. Tribes had not been exposed to the same diseases as the Europeans. So they did not have the same **immunity** that Europeans had built up over the years. Diseases, such as smallpox, swept through the tribes. These silent killers could wipe out a whole village in a matter of days.

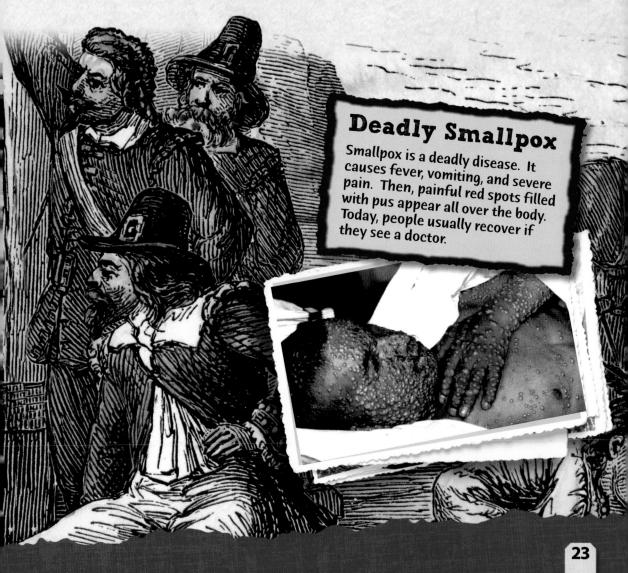

Deadly Smallpox

Smallpox is a deadly disease. It causes fever, vomiting, and severe pain. Then, painful red spots filled with pus appear all over the body. Today, people usually recover if they see a doctor.

Trade was not the only thing Europeans were after in the New World. Many came to gain more wealth and land for their home countries. The Spanish set up a vast empire in the New World. It stretched from California to Florida, and it contained much of South America. They destroyed many native villages and cultures in search of gold and silver. As they conquered more land, they also set up **missions** to **convert** the tribes to Catholicism. This was the religion of Spain and many other European countries.

Old West Mission San Jose in San Antonio, Texas

The Spanish forced tribes to live at the missions and to work as slaves. They did farm work and many other chores. The Spanish made them live and dress like the Spanish. Many American Indians struggled to adjust to life on a mission. If they disobeyed, the Spanish punished them harshly. Still, many resisted. They held on to their own beliefs.

As Europeans claimed more and more land, American Indians were pushed out of their homelands. Yet many tribes endured. Today, there are over five million American Indians living in the United States.

American Indians are portrayed greeting Spanish priests at a mission in California.

Keeping Their Cultures Alive

Many tribes still live in the West. But today, they live quite differently from how they did long ago. Today, most live in modern houses and wear modern clothing. They attend school and many go to college. They are teachers and doctors. They are writers and artists. They have their own businesses. Some American Indians live on **reservations**. These are like small countries inside the United States. There, tribal leaders make laws and decisions for their people. Other American Indians choose to live elsewhere. They live in cities and towns with other Americans.

American Indian pottery

The Navajo reservation is in parts of Utah, Arizona, and New Mexico.

ENTERING NAVAJO RESERVATION U.S. DEPT. INTERIOR

The San Manuel Indians hold their annual powwow in San Bernardino, California.

Many tribes hold traditional celebrations. They perform traditional dances. They use traditional cooking methods. They make pottery and baskets like their ancestors did long ago. Many have held onto their tribal beliefs. Some still speak their tribal languages. They try to teach others about their cultures.

American Indians were the first Americans. Their ancestors came to this land long ago. Those who lived in the West battled the elements. They faced many challenges when Europeans arrived. As a people, they survived it all. Today, these tribes proudly keep their traditions alive.

Research It!

Research a specific tribe from the West. The tribe may be one from this book or not. Identify what the people wore, what they ate, the type of home they lived in, their religious beliefs, whether they were nomadic or lived in permanent settlements, and details about their daily lives. Investigate where the tribe is today and how the people's lives have changed. Then, write and illustrate a picture book to show what you learned. Read your book to your friends or family members. Teach them about the tribe.

Glossary

ancestors—people that a group is descended from

Columbian Exchange—the trading of plants, animals, and ideas between the New and Old Worlds

convert—to change from one religion or belief to another

culture—beliefs and ways of a group of people

descendants—people who are related to groups of people from the past

diverse—made up of things that are different from each other

immunity—the body's ability to fight off infection from a disease

missions—buildings where religious work is done

nomadic—lifestyle where groups of people move from place to place and have no permanent home

opportunity—chance to progress or move forward

pueblos—homes with flat roofs that were made by Southwest American Indian tribes

reservations—areas of land in the United States that are kept separate as places for American Indians to live

temporary—lasting for a short time; not permanent

tribes—groups of people who have the same language, customs, and beliefs

unique—unlike anything else

Index

Your Turn!

Pueblo Home

American Indians in the Southwest often lived in pueblos like this one. How is this type of home suited to the environment in the Southwest? Why didn't tribes in other regions live in pueblos? Write a paragraph using examples to describe how location affected the types of homes different tribes built.